AFRICAN AMERICAN FOLK SONGS
COLLECTION

24 Traditional Folk Songs for Intermediate Piano Solo

ARRANGED BY ARTINA McCAIN

ISBN 978-1-70511-470-4

Visit Hal Leonard Online at
www.halleonard.com

Contact us:
Hal Leonard
7777 West Bluemound Road
Milwaukee, WI 53213
Email: info@halleonard.com

In Europe, contact:
Hal Leonard Europe Limited
42 Wigmore Street
Marylebone, London, W1U 2RN
Email: info@halleonardeurope.com

In Australia, contact:
Hal Leonard Australia Pty. Ltd.
4 Lentara Court
Cheltenham, Victoria, 3192 Australia
Email: info@halleonard.com.au

FROM THE ARRANGER

African Americans[1] created a rich history of song and dance. I am proud to say that I am the great-great-great-granddaughter of these strong and resilient enslaved Americans and can trace my origins in America back almost 200 years. In the late 18th century our musical history began with the African American Spiritual (or Negro Spiritual) and is the largest and most significant form of American folk song. There are over 6000 of these anonymous masterpieces! Through oral tradition, they were passed down from generation to generation and brilliantly blended the rich musical culture of Africa, with text describing hardships that they were experiencing in America.[2]

Spirituals can be organized into three categories: code or protest songs, sorrow songs, and jubilee songs. They hold messages of hope, resilience, and the strong identification of their own lives with fascinating parallels to biblical stories. Frederick Douglass, among others, celebrated the genius of these songs. In his book *Narrative of the Life of Frederick Douglass, an American Slave* he wrote: "…every tone was a testimony against slavery, and a prayer to God for deliverance from chains." In 1871, the Jubilee Singers from Fisk University, who were former slaves, were the first group to collect, perform, and record these songs for the public. They were followed by a wave of other composers who arranged and performed these spirituals.

A few include Harry T. Burleigh, Roland Hayes, R. Nathaniel Dett, and Samuel Coleridge-Taylor. Now numerous composers, artists, and arrangers have a fascination with these melodious, sorrowful, and joyful songs.

In this book, I explored some of the most popular spirituals, along with a few other African American folk songs that originated from West Africa. As an African American, the spiritual is very meaningful for me. One common aspect of the spiritual is call and response. A leader will sing a verse and a congregational chorus of singers will respond in refrain. While growing up, I had a front row seat to watch and experience call and response. My grandfather lead the call and response in his church to hymns and spirituals during devotional time. My grandmother played piano and sung in the choir. As a kid, these seemed like "old folk" songs, but the creation of this book has taken me on a deeper dive into the research and historical meanings of these important songs.

The process of notating these spirituals for the intermediate level pianist has been deeply gratifying. Thanks so much to Charmaine Siagian for the invitation to share these pieces with you! I hope that this book will spark your curiosity to learn more about the wonderful history of these spirituals and other traditional songs by African Americans.

[1] Referring to those who are descendants of American slavery.
[2] For more information, visit https://www.loc.gov/item/ihas.200197495/.

ABOUT THE ARRANGER

Artina McCain was born in Arlington, Texas and graduated *cum laude* from Southern Methodist University. In 2010, she recorded an award-winning album of African American spirituals and art songs with soprano Icy Simpson. Over the span of her performance career she has dedicated herself to performing, recording, and teaching the works of composers of African descent. Dr. McCain has won multiple Global Music Awards and an American Prize for her recordings of these works for solo and chamber music: *I, Too* (voice/piano), *Heritage* (solo piano) and *Shades* (trombone/piano). She received her Master of Music from Cleveland Institute of Music and holds a doctoral degree from the University of Texas at Austin. Currently she is a professor, independent pedagogue, and concert artist based in Memphis, Tennessee.

TABLE OF CONTENTS

NOTES ON THE AFRICAN AMERICAN FOLK SONGS

LITTLE DAVID, PLAY ON YOUR HARP (page 8)
This jubilee tells the biblical story of David—a masterful musician, king, and slayer of the giant Goliath. The LH should imitate David strumming sounds on the harp, while the right hand sings the text "Little David, play on your harp, hallelu, hallelu" with overwhelming joy.

GUIDE MY FEET (page 9)
The author is pleading for divine intervention and wisdom while navigating the hard times in life. This sorrow song has been sung during times that African Americans faced racial hardships in the 20th and 21st century. Each time the verse is repeated it asks for the Lord's guidance: "Guide my feet..., hold my hand...., stand by me..." etc.

DIDN'T MY LORD DELIVER DANIEL (page 10)
This code spiritual reminded enslaved people that if the Lord delivered Daniel from a lions' den, he could deliver them too!: "Didn't my Lord deliver Daniel, deliver Daniel, deliver Daniel...and why not every man?"

WADE IN THE WATER (page 11)
"Wade in the Water" is a code spiritual with a double meaning. Enslaved people longed for freedom and created songs telling each other the paths to take in order to escape to free states. "Wade in the Water" was one of those songs that helped lead people to freedom. The lyric "Wade in the water, God's gonna trouble the water" also refers to God providing healing (see John 5:4).

WARRIORS' SONG (page 12)
"Warriors' Song" is one of several songs originally notated by a Swiss missionary, Henri Junod (1863-1934), in a book called *Introduction and the Songs of the Ba-Ronga*. Ronga is in modern-day Mozambique. This is one of many tunes that was brought to the US during the trans-Atlantic slave trade.

SOMETIMES I FEEL LIKE A MOTHERLESS CHILD (page 13)
A sorrow song that reflects the unfortunate reality during slavery times of humans being separated from their family. This occurred often with the sale or transfer of family member(s) to another plantation. It laments: "Sometimes I feel like a motherless child, a long way from home."

BY AND BY (page 14)
This sorrow song is full of encouragement. Despite the constant troubles during the civil rights movement, this became one of the many anthems adapted from the spirituals' era. The text states that we will understand the woes of the world little by little or after we reach the promised land. Here the promised land refers to heaven or the afterlife: "By and by when the morning comes, when the saints of God are gathered home, we'll tell the story of how we overcome, and we'll understand it better by and by."

My Lord, What a Morning (page 16)

This is a spiritual that provides encouragement for better days. It proclaims of a day when slaves will be free, whether in death or emancipation. The lyrics proclaim: "My Lord, what a morning!—when the stars begin to fall."

Take Nabandji (page 17)

Like "Warriors' Song," this was also notated by Swiss missionary Henri Junod and brought to the United States during the trans-Atlantic slave trade.

Song of Conquest (page 18)

A folk song that originates from the Igbo (now Ebo) people from southeastern Nigeria, one of the largest ethnic groups in Africa.

Don't You Let Nobody Turn You Around (page 20)

Originally a Negro Spiritual, this was adapted during the civil rights era by Reverend Ralph Abernathy (1926-90) as a protest song. It is typically performed and sung with rhythmic clapping and singing: "Don't you let nobody turn you 'round, turn you 'round, turn you 'round – you got to keep on walkin', keep on talkin', marchin' to the freedom land."

Run, Mary, Run (page 21)

This is another code song that encouraged enslaved people to run to freedom. In this song they use the name "Mary" from the Bible, most likely to encourage the enslaved person to have faith on what is sure to be a perilous journey.

Give Me That Old Time Religion (page 22)

This beloved jubilee song dates to 1873 (or earlier). It was first popularized by the Fisk Jubilee Singers and was commonly performed with clapping and dancing.

Every Time I Feel the Spirit (page 24)

This is a jubilee spiritual that evokes feelings of joy and exuberance. The author exclaims, "Every time I feel the Spirit moving in my heart I will pray," meaning the spirit guides them to act in their daily life.

Deep River (page 26)

Considered one of the sorrow or code songs, this tune expresses a desire for freedom on earth and the afterlife. It's a slow, thoughtful melody full of hope and expectation for a better tomorrow. This was another one of the many spirituals championed by the Fisk Jubilee Singers after the end of slavery in the 1870's: "Deep river, my home is over Jordan."

I Want Jesus to Walk With Me (page 28)

This song of lament, invitation, and assurance describes Jesus walking with those that suffer. It is also considered a journey or a sorrow song that describes God as a companion along life's journey.

I Was Way Down a-Yonder (page 30)

This spiritual is a sorrow song that describes yearning for an eternal better day: "Way down yonder in the graveyard walk, I thank God I'm free at last."

I'M A SOLDIER, LET ME RIDE (page 32)

Originally, this spiritual was called either "Slow Down, Sweet Chariot and Let Me Ride" or "Swing Down, Chariot, Stop and Let Me Ride." It would have included stomping and clapping instead of drums, since those were banned during slavery. This song was also performed and popularized by the Fisk Jubilee singers.

WATCH AND PRAY (page 33)

"Watch and Pray" is a spiritual sung from the vantage point of a child that is potentially being sold into slavery. They ask their mother to watch and pray for a different outcome and for the grief to be comforted: "Mama, is Massa (master) goin' to sell us tomorrow? Yes, yes, yes. Oh, watch and pray."

THE BAMBOULA (page 34)

A *bamboula* is a drum that is covered with skin made from bamboo and used for dancing and singing. It originated in West Africa and was used by enslaved people in America. This music would be accompanied by a lively, sensuous, and rhythmic bamboula dance.

WHAT A BEAUTIFUL CITY (page 36)

This jubilee piece describes heaven and the beautiful city that awaits those that believe: "Oh, what a beautiful city, twelve gates to the city, hallelujah."

RIDE ON, KING JESUS (page 39)

Many enslaved African Americans identified with Bible stories and Christ's suffering and resurrection in a very tangible way. If Christ could overcome his suffering, so could they. The lyrics state: "He is the King of Kings, He is the Lord of Lords, Jesus Christ, the First and Last, no man can a-hinder me, no man can a-hinder me."

IN BRIGHT MANSIONS ABOVE (page 42)

This is yet another spiritual about beauty and joy in the afterlife. The song speaks of reuniting with family members and beautiful mansions in paradise: "In bright mansions above, Lord, I wan' t' go there too, Lord, I wan' t' live up yonder, in bright mansions above."

LIFT EV'RY VOICE AND SING (page 46)

This is known as the Black (or African American) national anthem. The poem was written by James Weldon Johnson and the music by his brother John Rosamond Johnson in 1900. The song became a rallying cry during the civil rights movement in the 1950s and 60s. The poetry explores themes of freedom achieved and suffering overcome by African Americans. It embodies joy and acknowledges the accomplishments of our ancestors, while alluding to work yet to be done: "Lift every voice and sing till earth and heaven ring, Ring with the harmonies of Liberty, Let our rejoicing rise high as the listening skies, Let it resound loud as the rolling sea." The complete lyrics are provided on page 45.

Little David, Play on Your Harp

Traditional
Arranged by Artina McCain

Playful and light (♩ = c. 100)

GUIDE MY FEET

African American Spiritual
Arranged by Artina McCain

Joyfully (♩ = c. 50)

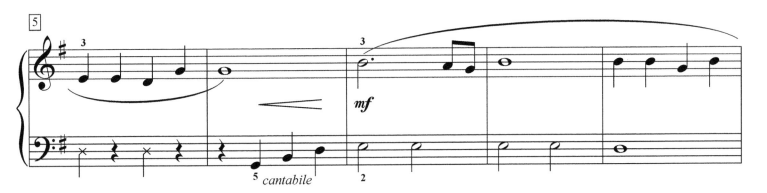

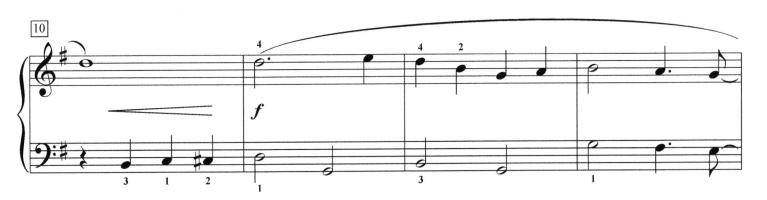

Didn't My Lord Deliver Daniel

African American Spiritual
Arranged by Artina McCain

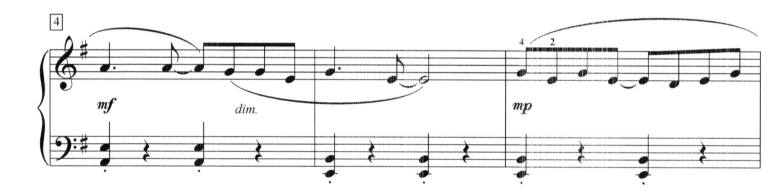

WADE IN THE WATER

Traditional Spiritual
Arranged by Artina McCain

Warriors' Song

African American Folk Song
Arranged by Artina McCain

Sometimes I Feel Like a Motherless Child

African American Spiritual
Arranged by Artina McCain

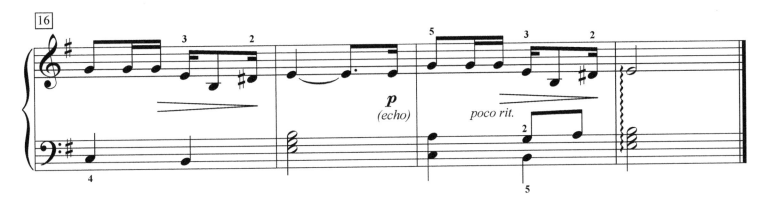

By and By

Traditional
Arranged by Artina McCain

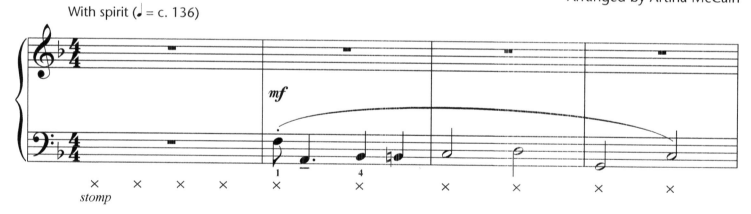

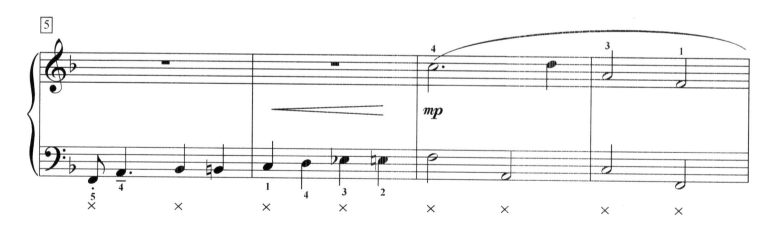

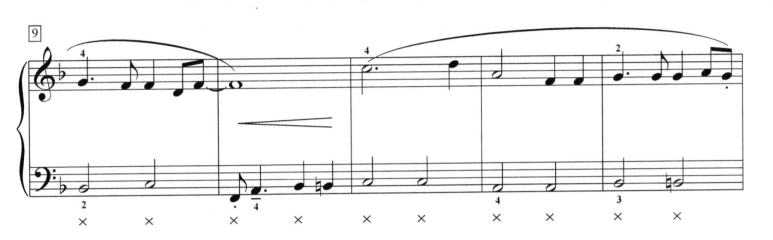

MY LORD, WHAT A MORNING

African American Spiritual
Arranged by Artina McCain

Take Nabandji

African American Folk Song
Arranged by Artina McCain

Urgent, with purpose (♩ = 80)

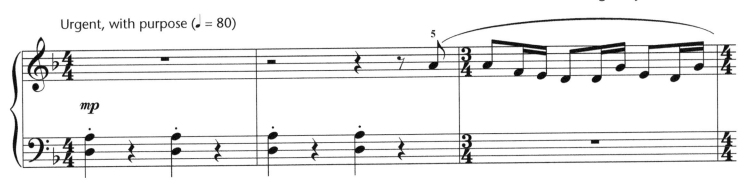

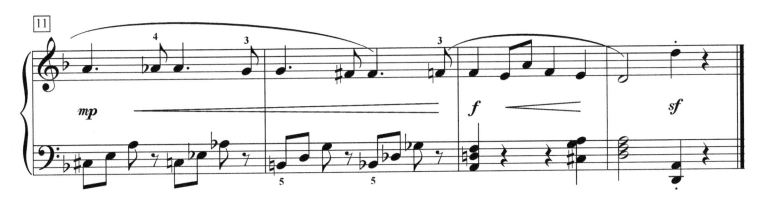

SONG OF CONQUEST

African American Folk Song
Arranged by Artina McCain

Joyful (♩. = c. 92)

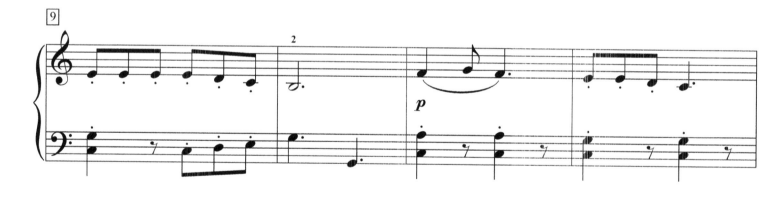

Slower (♩. = 72)

Don't You Let Nobody Turn You Around

African American Spiritual
Arranged by Artina McCain

Play with determination (♩ = c. 70)

RUN, MARY, RUN

Traditional Spiritual
Arranged by Artina McCain

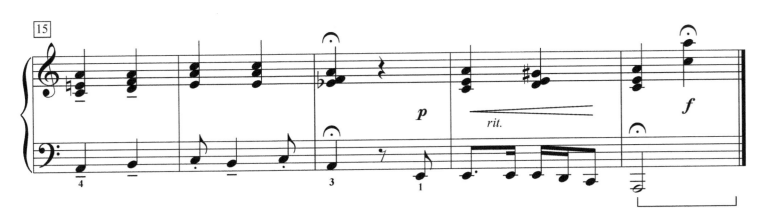

GIVE ME THAT OLD TIME RELIGION

Traditional
Arranged by Artina McCain

[Set metronome for beats 2 and 4]

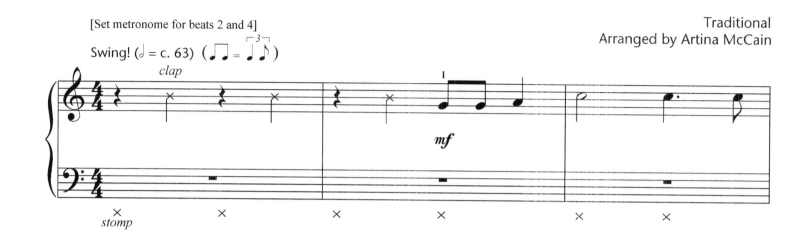

L.H. legato

Every Time I Feel the Spirit

African American Spiritual
Arranged by Artina McCain

With joy (♩ = c. 148)

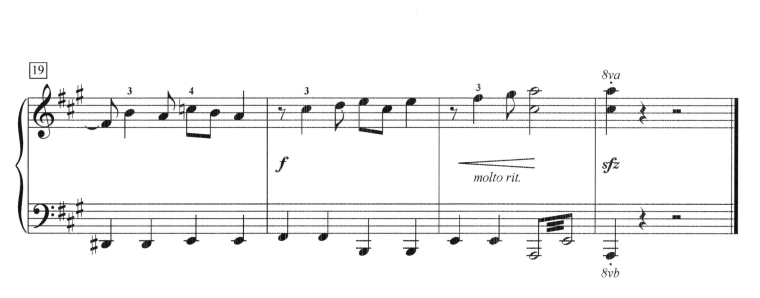

DEEP RIVER

African American Spiritual
Arranged by Artina McCain

I Want Jesus to Walk with Me

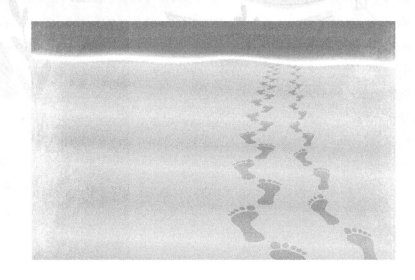

African American Spiritual
Arranged by Artina McCain

I Was Way Down A-Yonder

African American Spiritual
Arranged by Artina McCain

Tempo I, triumphantly

I'm a Soldier, Let Me Ride

African American Spiritual
Arranged by Artina McCain

Watch and Pray

African American Spiritual
Arranged by Artina McCain

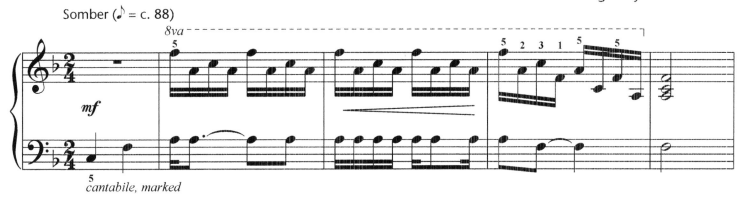

THE BAMBOULA

African American Folk Song
Arranged by Artina McCain

Playful, dance-like (♩ = c. 70)

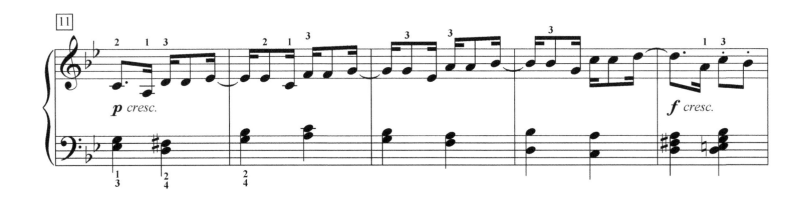

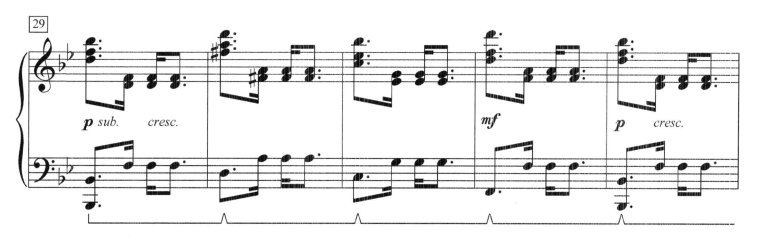

WHAT A BEAUTIFUL CITY

African American Spiritual
Arranged by Artina McCain

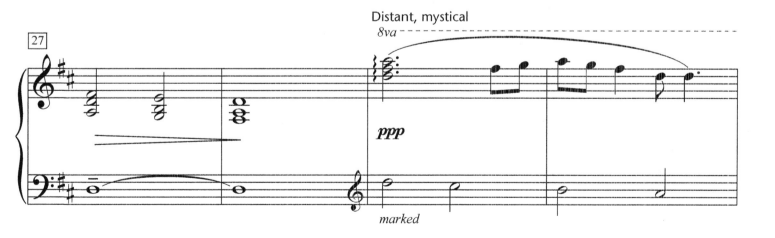

Ride On, King Jesus

African American Spiritual
Arranged by Artina McCain

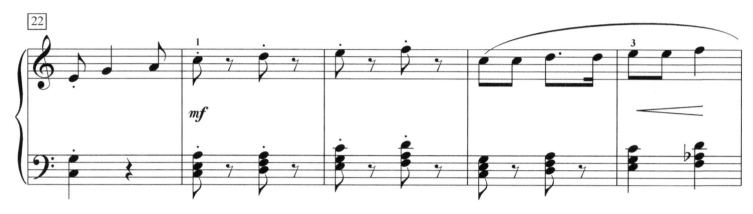

L.H. bell-like

IN BRIGHT MANSIONS ABOVE

African American Spiritual
Arranged by Artina McCain

Gentle and dreamy (♩ = c. 54)

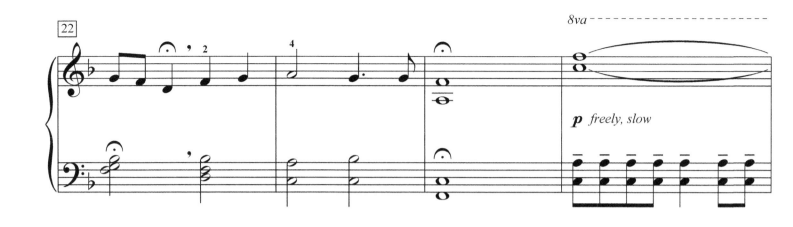

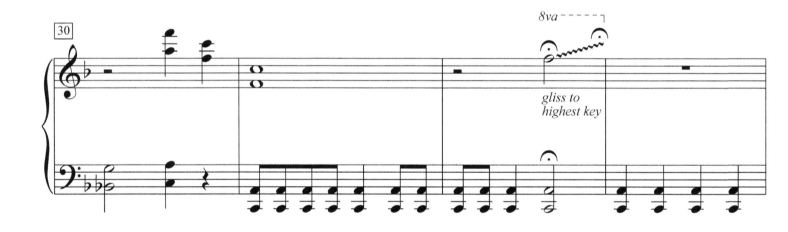

LIFT EV'RY VOICE

By James Weldon Johnson

Lift ev'ry voice and sing,
Till earth and heaven ring,
Ring with the harmonies of Liberty;
Let our rejoicing rise
High as the list'ning skies,
Let it resound loud as the rolling sea.
Sing a song full of the faith that the dark past has taught us,
Sing a song full of the hope that the present has brought us;
Facing the rising sun of our new day begun,
Let us march on till victory is won.

Stony the road we trod,
Bitter the chast'ning rod,
Felt in the days when hope unborn had died;
Yet with a steady beat,
Have not our weary feet
Come to the place for which our fathers sighed?
We have come over a way that with tears has been watered,
We have come, treading our path through the blood of the slaughtered,
Out from the gloomy past,
Till now we stand at last
Where the white gleam of our bright star is cast.

God of our weary years,
God of our silent tears,
Thou who has brought us thus far on the way;
Thou who has by Thy might,
Led us into the light,
Keep us forever in the path, we pray.
Lest our feet stray from the places, our God, where we met Thee,
Lest our hearts, drunk with the wine of the world, we forget Thee;
Shadowed beneath Thy hand,
May we forever stand.
True to our God,
True to our native land.

Lift Ev'ry Voice and Sing

Words by James Weldon Johnson
Music by J. Rosamond Johnson
Arranged by Artina McCain

FOLK SONG COLLECTIONS
FOR PIANO

Introduce piano students to the music of world cultures with these folk songs arranged for intermediate piano solo. Each collection features 24 folk songs and includes detailed notes about the folk songs, beautiful illustrations, as well as a map of the regions.

AFRICAN AMERICAN FOLK SONGS COLLECTION
24 TRADITIONAL FOLK SONGS FOR
INTERMEDIATE LEVEL PIANO SOLO | *arr. Artina McCain*

The Bamboula • By and By • Deep River • Didn't My Lord Deliver Daniel? • Don't You Let Nobody Turn You Around • Every Time I Feel the Spirit • Give Me That Old Time Religion • Guide My Feet • I Want Jesus to Walk With Me • I Was Way Down A-Yonder • I'm a Soldier, Let Me Ride • In Bright Mansions Above • Lift Ev'ry Voice and Sing • Little David, Play on Your Harp • My Lord, What a Morning • Ride On, King Jesus • Run Mary Run • Sometimes I Feel Like a Motherless Child • Song of Conquest • Take Nabandji • Wade in the Water • Warriors' Song • Watch and Pray • What a Beautiful City.
00358084 Piano Solo..$12.99

IRISH FOLK SONGS COLLECTION
24 TRADITIONAL FOLK SONGS FOR
INTERMEDIATE LEVEL PIANO SOLO | *arr. June Armstrong*

As I Walked Out One Morning • Ballinderry • Blind Mary • Bunclody • Carrickfergus • The Castle of Dromore (The October Winds) • The Cliffs of Doneen • The Coolin • Courtin' in the Kitchen • Down Among the Ditches O • Down by the Salley Gardens • The Fairy Woman of Lough Leane • Follow Me Up to Carlow • The Gartan Mother's Lullaby • Huish the Cat • I'll Tell My Ma • Kitty of Coleraine • The Londonderry Air • My Lagan Love • My Love Is an Arbutus • Rocky Road to Dublin • Slieve Gallion Braes • Squire Parsons • That Night in Bethlehem.
00234359 Piano Solo.. $9.99

MALAY FOLK SONGS COLLECTION
24 TRADITIONAL SONGS ARRANGED FOR
INTERMEDIATE LEVEL PIANO SOLO | *arr. Charmaine Siagian*

At Dawn • Chan Mali Chan • C'mon, Mama! • The Cockatoo • The Curvy Water Spinach Stalk • Five Little Chicks • God Bless the Sultan • The Goodbye Song • Great Indonesia • It's All Good Here • The Jumping Frog • Longing • Mak Inang • Milk Coffee • The Moon Kite • Morning Tide • My Country • Onward Singapore • Ponyfish • Song for the Ladybugs • The Stork Song • Suriram • Trek Tek Tek • Voyage of the Sampan.
00288420 Piano Solo.. $10.99

CHINESE FOLK SONGS COLLECTION
24 TRADITIONAL SONGS ARRANGED FOR
INTERMEDIATE LEVEL PIANO SOLO | *arr. Joseph Johnson*

Beating the Wild Hog • Blue Flower • Carrying Song • Crescent Moon • Darkening Sky • Digging for Potatoes • Girl's Lament • Great Wall • Hand Drum Song • Homesick • Jasmine Flower Song • Little Cowherd • Love Song of the Prarie • Memorial • Mountaintop View • Northwest Rains • Running Horse Mountain • Sad, Rainy Day • Song of the Clown • The Sun Came Up Happy • Wa-Ha-Ha • Wedding Veil • White Flower • Woven Basket.
00296764 Piano Solo...$10.99

KOREAN FOLK SONGS COLLECTION
24 TRADITIONAL FOLK SONGS FOR
INTERMEDIATE LEVEL PIANO SOLO | *arr. Lawrence Lee*

Arirang • Autumn in the City • Birdie, Birdie • Boat Song • Catch the Tail • Chestnut • Cricket • Dance in the Moonlight • Five Hundred Years • Flowers • Fun Is Here • The Gate • Han River • Harvest • Jindo Field Song • Lullaby • The Mill • The Palace • The Pier • Three-Way Junction • Waterfall • Wild Herbs • Yearning • You and I.
00296810 Piano Solo...$10.99

JAPANESE FOLK SONGS COLLECTION
24 TRADITIONAL FOLK SONGS FOR
INTERMEDIATE LEVEL PIANO SOLO | *arr. Mika Goto*

Blooming Flowers • Come Here, Fireflies • Counting Game • The Fisherman's Song • Going to the Shrine • Harvest Song • Itsuki Lullaby • Joyful Doll Festival • Kimigayo • Let's Sing • My Hometown • Picking Tea Leaves • The Rabbit on the Moon • Rain • Rain Showers • Rock-Paper-Scissors • Sakura • Seven Baby Crows • Takeda Lullaby • Time to Go Home • Village Festival • Where Are You From? • Wish I Could Go • You're It!
00296891 Piano Solo...$9.99

halleonard.com

0721
067

Prices, contents and availability subject to change without notice.